# Insanely Great:  A Steve Jobs Biography

## Introduction

People who change the world are polarizing figures who leave their marks on history for better or for worse.  Their efforts are the evidence of humans as a force of nature that is not unlike bodies of water that carve deep channels into seemingly indestructible formations of rock.  Like it or not, we cannot deny that these people set the trend for generations to come.  These are people who create civilizations, introduce science to society, invent the written word, and determine the destiny of future generations.

At the risk of sounding grandiose, we are nonetheless compelled to think that Steve Jobs is undoubtedly one of those figures, someone who is more of a legend than a human being.  Even after death, Jobs continues to change our world.  Odds are that if you reach into your pocket, you will touch a piece of your life that would not exist without him.  You use this item every day and you take it with you wherever you go, whether it be school, work, your gym, at a date with your partner, at a bar with friends, or even when just lounging on the couch. You use this item to listen to music, make phone calls, browse Wikipedia, Twitter, and Facebook. It could even be what you use to write that novel you have always told your friends and family you'll do when you get around to it.

We take these devices for granted and often do not give them a second thought. But today, we cannot live without them. They are vital components of our lives and the world in which we live in. All of that would not have existed without two unassuming young men tinkering with electronics in a garage long ago.

Steve Jobs is the epitome of capitalism, rising from a college drop out to the founder and CEO of an empire that is unparalleled in recent history. His work is all around us, and it is now a part of who we are.

But Jobs was also an incredibly flawed man; a human with some qualities that go against decency. His perfectionism made him an unforgiving taskmaster to his employees, who worked night and day to see his remarkable visions come true.

Jobs failed his loved ones throughout his life. When it came to both his career and personal life, he often placed himself above others and dismissed the importance of those who worked with him. Amazing as he was at what he did, he could not easily navigate relationships with individuals nor engage in polite conversation. These problems are typical for those who believe they have no peers. Even if they soar to the greatest heights, they are likewise removed from those on the ground.

This is not to say that Steve Jobs was a bad person. If we could see into the lives of his critics, we would undoubtedly see the same failures, just in varying degrees. Indeed, if we look into the personal lives of other game changers—advocates for civil rights, political leaders, artists, writers, and other icons—we can see the same pride, the same self-sense of superiority and the same ugliness.

But the same could be said for everyone, including this author, who writes using an invention that would not exist without the subject of this piece. Although he was myopic when it came to the importance of working with people, he also worked on himself as he did his projects. Like many great people, he came to see that he was less than perfect, and when faced with that imperfection, he looked the beast in the eye and dared to change himself in the same way he changed the world.

## Childhood

Jobs was the child of a returning US Coast Guard officer and the daughter of immigrants fleeing from Turkey in the wake of the Armenian genocide. His father, Paul, joined the Coast Guard when he was nineteen, and after the end of World War II, came home on a bet with his fellow veterans that he would be married in two weeks. His friends laughed at the idea, but Paul had the last laugh.

Ten days later in March of 1946, he married Clara, a widow whose husband had been killed in the war.

Despite the fact that they did not know much about each other when they were wed, Paul and Clara were reportedly happy and they got along remarkably well considering they were practically strangers. They got by thanks to Paul's vocation as a machinist and his inherent ingenuity with buying parts and selling them for higher prices. The income was small, but it was enough for them to live independently.

Soon after they were married, they decided to have children and raise a family. However, that proved difficult for the happy couple.

Clara had a failed pregnancy in which the fetus could not fully enter her uterus, so they decided after nine years of marriage to adopt a child rather than continue trying to conceive naturally. This was how they acquired the infant Steve, their first child.

Jobs' origins make for a lengthy story in addition to the one of his adult life. His biological parents were Joanne Shieble, a young woman from a strict Catholic family and Abdulfattah "John" Jandali, who was the youngest child of a Muslim from Syria. They were roughly the same age, and Joanne, 23, discovered that she was pregnant with Jandali's child. The couple had problems before Jobs' conception and the pregnancy broke up their already troubled relationship.

Jandali refused to stay in the relationship when he was confronted with fatherhood. The irony was that Jobs himself would one day be confronted with the same situation, and he would react to it the same way Jandali did. Even in real life, stories sometimes play out like the spoke of wheel returning to the same place where it began.

Joanne's family left her in a predicament that she could not escape from. Her father said he would disown her if she married or had a child with a man of a different religion. There was no problem with race, but religion put Joanne in a bind. She could not live independently and she did not have the means necessary to raise a child. So, with immense reluctance, she gave her baby up for adoption. The infant who would become Steve Jobs was born on February 24, 1955.

Initially, there was friction between Joanne, Paul and Clara because Steve's biological mother wanted her child to be raised by college graduates. However, when Jobs' original foster parents returned him to Joanne's doctor because they wanted a girl, the baby was lost in a mix-up. Joanne eventually relented on the proviso that the baby's adopted family would open a bank account to pay for his college education. When the two parties agreed to these terms, Steve was given to Paul and Clara.

The knowledge of his adoption played no small part in forming young Steve Jobs' personality. Growing up, Jobs had to adjust to the fact he was an adopted child, and it was clearly more difficult for him then he let on. When young Jobs learned that he was adopted, he broke down in tears. He recovered from that trauma, and would go on to have a loving relationship with his parents, especially with his father.

However, the truth was hard for him to swallow because he perceived himself as a sole individual with no immediate connection to anyone. This dilemma did provide him with the opportunity to reframe the history of his birth and adoption into a narrative that lent him power. Because he was adopted and apart from anyone else, he was "chosen" and "special". As he grew older, he prided himself with this newfound sense of self and as an independent orphan who could conquer the world through sheer willpower.

This approach to life was not without its drawbacks.

Despite his obviously gifted intellect, Steve nevertheless was at odds with fellow students and teachers. He did not do well at school and was a natural loner who tended to drive others away. He seemed to be a hopeless case because no one was able to get him to yield to the norm. But, despite all these problems, Jobs' trouble with education began to turn around after 3rd grade. Patient teachers knew that they could not overpower Jobs because he was an intellectual and emotional juggernaut, so the only way to teach him was to appeal to his sense of uniqueness.

That is exactly what his 4th grade teacher did: by attracting his intellect rather than trying to control it. "She taught an advanced 4th grade class and it took her about a month to get hip to my situation," Jobs recounted. "She bribed me into learning. She would say, 'I really want you to finish this workbook. I'll give you five bucks if you finish.' That really kindled a passion in me for learning things! I'll give you five bucks if you finish it.' I learned more that year than I think I learned in any other year in school." With a new mentality, Jobs began to thrive in the classroom environment and became unparalleled as a student, albeit one who could only work alone and not on a team. Nonetheless, his new enthusiasm, combined with his intellect and zest, caught the attention of teachers working with him. "They wanted me to skip the next two years in grade school and go straight to junior high to learn a foreign language but my parents very wisely wouldn't let it happen."

Jobs' parents tried very hard to ground him in his education in order to keep his pride in check. Jobs' self-image of independence—the idea that— because he was special, he was better than anyone else—was apparent early on. His parents addressed this problem with little success, and Jobs' life suffered as a result, even though it proved invaluable for his personal development and career. In his eyes, if people were not helpful then people were useless.

Subsequently, he became controlling when he performed tasks with others. The latter quality distanced himself from family and friends and created problems for him at work. His virtue was a mixed bag, but, without it, he could not have been the game-changer he would later become. The confidence he embodied was a weapon that allowed him to go farther than most and made him a great businessman as well as an engineer and designer.

His one saving grace was his family.

As a child, Jobs was very close to his father, who was handy at fixing things around the house and who contributed to Jobs' college fund by buying used cars, remodeling them, and then selling them for more money than what he spent on them. Even though Steve was not attracted to the same work as his father, he did not shirk spending time with him and helping him with updates to the house, like rebuilding the fence.

Although Jobs vehemently denied that being adopted drove him to be close to his parents, people close to him thought this was not so. Later on, when he had a daughter with Chrisann Brennan, Jobs refused to have anything to do with the matter. He even denied that the child was his. "He who is abandoned is an abandoner," Brennan went on to say. Colleague Andy Hertzfield also entertained the idea that being abandoned is what drove Jobs to such aversive and cruel behavior. However, he later rectified the situation and began paying child support and in addition paid the state of California for the years he had withheld money when he removed himself from his child's life.

At school, Jobs had a reputation of being a trouble-maker. He balked at the authority the teachers tried to impose on him and recounted that he was glad that they didn't drive his inherent curiosity out of him. This trait in his personality was a virtue as well as a vice for himself and others—he made himself the only authority to which he answered. So it is no surprise that he was without remorse when he chastised employees in all the years he worked at Apple. This came from an inherent sense of entitlement and perfectionism that produced magnificent outcomes but also was not without its drawbacks. He displayed little concern for others outside of what they could do, and the geniuses who worked for him would mostly go nameless and not share in his legend. His audacity to rebel against authority figures went hand-in-hand with the gulf that would separate him from others. Of all the feats Jobs would accomplish, none of them would come close to his growth as a human being, who would be complete in heart as well as in mind.

## High School

At his high school near Silicon Valley, Jobs clashed with teachers and let his hair grow long as he became a part of the counter-culture movement that began in the 1970's. During this time, he began using marijuana and pursued education outside of traditional school. He was an adept student in science and engineering and expanded his interests to include greek philosophy, literature, and creative writing. He devoured the writings of Plato and Shakespeare, and he firmly believed in strengthening his independence along with his intellect. For the young Jobs, there would be no distinction between the two.

Although Jobs took on the likeness of a hippie, he was not a part of any group or club, aside from his friendship with Steve Wozniak, who was at Stanford at the time. By all appearances, Jobs was purely an individual, self-absorbed and completely apart from people in general. While this quality alienated many, it allowed Jobs to work on his inner-self and adopt a unique position in both his personal and professional life.

## Coming of Age

Jobs attended Reed College in 1972. When his parents pulled up in front of the campus, he set out with fearless determination, ready to take on what lay ahead. But he didn't say goodbye to his parents, the people who had taken care of him with utmost love and tenderness. On the surface, the absence of acknowledgement would seem strange even of Jobs. After all, he had no serious problems between himself and the people who raised him. But as we noted earlier, Jobs thrived on the idea that he was independent and special. This complex may have sustained the health of his psyche after he discovered he was adopted, but it was also a vice which lent him a sense of entitlement letting him think that he was better than others. His ability to overcome challenges without hesitation was clearly tied with his lack of consideration of other people, even those closest to him. Years later, he expressed no small amount of remorse over the incident. "It's one of the things in life I really feel ashamed about. I was not very sensitive, and I hurt their feelings. I shouldn't have . . . I didn't want anyone to know I had parents. I wanted to be like an orphan who had bummed around the country on trains and just arrived out of nowhere, with no roots, no connection, no background."

## Spiritual Influences

When he dropped out of college in 1974, Jobs became deeply involved in Zen Buddhism and travelled to India. In his travels, he experimented with LSD and other psychedelics and went so far as to shave his head and adopt eastern attire. Jobs stated that these were among the most important experiences of his life and they enhanced his creativity. This apparent connection between spirituality and advanced science serves as a fascinating example of the counterintuitive dependence of mind and spirit. Indeed, the idea that innovation of computer technology has to be cold, removed and purely logical does not work in real life. Looking closely, one can see the personality instilled in the technology of Jobs' legacy. Steve Jobs was many things good and bad, but, above all, he was among the few who saw that technology required a sense of personality.

## Work Life

"I was lucky to get into computers when it was a very young and idealistic industry," Jobs recounted. Unfortunately, computer science was not in vogue at that time since it was still in the domain of companies like IBM, which were not primarily concerned with the use of the computer in everyday life. Jobs had to approach the field from a sense of vocation rather than a desire to benefit financially. "There weren't many degrees offered in computer science, so people in computers were brilliant people from mathematics, physics, music, zoology, whatever. They loved it, and no one was really in it for the money."

Nevertheless, there were "people around here who start companies just to make money, but the great complainers, well, that's what they're about."

After India, Jobs began working at Atari. Although he was standoffish, he came into his own, someone who "was the smartest person in the room, and he would let you know it." His employer at Atari was often frustrated with Jobs because of his behavior and lack of compliance. However, he noted that Jobs was indispensable as much as he was problematic, an individual who was "difficult, but valuable". Jobs was clearly coming into his own.

But none of this changed the fact that Jobs' behavior was not only boorish, but reprehensible.

Even his one-time friend and colleague Steve Wozniak saw moments where Jobs was wanting in interpersonal skills, and Wozniak had to learn the hard way that Jobs was duplicitous.

When Jobs was given a task to make a simpler version of the video game Pong, he worked on the project with Wozniak and told him that he would give half of the money to Wozniak for his help. This proposition was a bold lie—Jobs was being paid a much higher price than what he told Wozniak the job would pay. Wozniak found out about Jobs' deceit years later after reading about their project in a book titled *Zap*, detailing the history of Atari. The revelation hurt him deeply. "I cried, I cried quite a bit, when I read that book," Wozniak recounted. The deception was exacerbated by the fact that Wozniak had put in an extraordinary effort to complete the job.  In his biopic *Steve Jobs*, renowned author Walter Isaacson wrote, "Jobs

said it had to be done in four days and with the fewest chips possible.  What

he hid from Wozniak was that the deadline was one that Jobs had imposed."

Some versions of the story suggest that Wozniak did practically all of

the work on the Atari project–an arduous task.


Apple and The Personal Computer

In his 1987 book on Jobs and Apple, Jeffrey Young offered the

following insight to capture how Jobs and Wozniak approached business.

"For what characterizes Apple is that its scientific staff always acted and

performed like artists—in a field filled with dry personalities limited by the

rational and binary worlds they inhabit, Apple's engineering teams had

passion.  They always believed that what they were doing was important and,

most of all, fun.  Working at Apple was never just a job; it was also a

crusade, a mission, to bring better computer power to people.  At its roots that

attitude came from Steve Jobs."  This personal touch in creating technology encapsulates how Jobs would define his career. It was an approach to a field that was otherwise governed by an image of a monolith of dry logic and lifeless intelligence, the kind pushes the everyday person away. Jobs and Wozniak's philosophy was that the average person should be able to incorporate the personal computer in their lives in the same way as they did with automobiles.

With Wozniak, Jobs worked hard to make the Apple I Computer. Their work paid off and the two Steves became household names when they created the Apple II, the most successful first mass-produced personal computer. It drew consumers into a new market and not only changed businesses and homes, but also how people imagined what computer technology could be. They were not challenged with an out-of-touch and intimidating piece of science and engineering; the computer had a face, and an appealing personality. Here was something that was as natural as it was remarkable, and everyone assimilated it into their lives with unexpected ease.

"Basically, Steve Wozniak and I invented the Apple because we wanted a personal computer. Not only couldn't we afford the computers on the market, those computers were impractical for us to use." Jobs saw how the computer technology of the time was cold and removed from the everyday person. He had insight that the only effective approach to any technology was to make it as personal as possible. "The Volkswagen isn't as fast or as comfortable as other ways of traveling, but the VW owners can go where they want, when they want and with whom they want. The VW owners have personal control of their car." Jobs soared with this unparalleled triumph that was equaled only by his lack of humanity on a personal level, even when, in 1977, he discovered that his on-again-off-again girlfriend was pregnant with his child.

Jobs' reaction to the news that he would be a father cannot be attributed to him being a "bad person". As brilliant as Jobs was, he had difficulty connecting with others. He was creative when he had to organize and manage other people to rethink problems and approached them with drive and ingenuity, but one-on-one, he simply could not connect with a friend or loved one in such a way as to make himself vulnerable, or what he most likely he saw as being powerless. We cannot reach back in time and read his mind, but it is not unreasonable to say that the prospect of emotional intimacy terrified him. If he could not govern a problem that involved only himself, with only his understanding and his independence, and not others *depending on him*, then he would most likely not approach it. This failure to initially take responsibility for his own child harkens back to the phrase "he who is abandoned is the abandoner". Again, the pattern of his behavior is illustrated by his origins: Jobs' biological parents gave him up and his biological father was the one who did not want any involvement.

His problems did not stop within his personal life—working for him was a nightmare.

One surreal and disturbing incident of abuse involved a job interview where Jobs asked the candidate inappropriate questions. What age did the candidate lose his virginity? When did he first try LSD? It is no surprise that the candidate left almost as soon as the interview began.

Incidents like these did not occur when Jobs just had a "bad moment". He was casual when it came to being mean-spirited and abusive. His best friend Jony Ive elaborated on the subject, saying that Jobs insisted that he did not stay mad. "I've claimed that Jobs was emotionally sensitive, and that he attained relief by treating others poorly, which in turn gave him a sense of power. And I think he feels he has a liberty and license to do that. The normal rules of social engagement, he feels, don't apply to him. Because of how very sensitive he is, he knows exactly how to efficiently and effectively hurt someone."

## Struggles within the Company

After a power struggle inside Apple pushed Jobs out, he went on to manage NeXT, which produced computers that changed the way companies were run and more importantly, sparked new life in the art and entertainment industries. Under Jobs' supervision, NeXT introduced computer-made graphic effects to Lucasfilm, an initiative that gave rise to Pixar. As a result, films and other forms of entertainment changed dramatically with the use of new visual effects and computer-generated imagery. Pixar introduced the world to *Toy Story*, whose success and iconography led to a new age of cartoons and other forms of animated entertainment. The film industry has never been the same—iconic characters and dramas exist in a new art form that expands versatility and allows filmmakers to take stories into new directions. None of this would have been possible without Jobs' creative and financial support.

With this new-found success, Jobs once again became the CEO of Apple when he merged it with NeXT. His intervention saved Apple from its lowest moment in 1997 when it faced bankruptcy and dissolution.

## Another Revolution

After the success of the Mac, Apple introduced the world to the first iPod in the early 2000's. To say this feat was an industry-changing event would be an understatement. In the place of bulky CD players, people could listen to songs of all genres from inside their pocket. These personal devices progressed with increasingly more storage space in smaller sizes throughout the 2000's.

Progress in this area led to the first iPhone in 2007. This would arguably be the greatest mark on Jobs' legacy and his best contribution to the world since the first personal computer he worked on with Wozniak three decades earlier. It also solidified his place in history and now it is what people know him best for. His feelings about the iPhone were evidently strong. "Every once in awhile, a product comes along that changes everything." Today's world could not agree with him more.

At this point, the cell phone became outdated with an unprecedented invention that was a phone and entertainment system all in one device that eventually surpassed the iPod. Newer models arrived and led to the iPad, which, although had a mixed reception at first, is taking the place of laptops in many functions. What direction Apple takes these inventions from here will be interesting to see.

## Death and Legacy

After a diagnosis of pancreatic cancer in 2003, Steve Jobs died in 2011. No one can say with pinpoint accuracy that Jobs was a "good" or "bad" person. Humans are too complex to fit into such black or white categories, and Jobs was far more complex than most people give him credit for. His life saw many twists and turns and ups and downs, and his relationships were troubled with his failure to completely grasp the interpersonal nature of human interactions. But he had the great virtue of persistence in the wake of failure and low expectations in his relationships. People are not set in stone, and they can change. Jobs was no different.

This is not to excuse many things Jobs did. "I think Apple goes out of its way to try to enhance his reputation and safeguard the 'great' Steve Jobs,"

Wozniak relented. However, Wozniak was also adamant that, although Jobs displayed less than desirable qualities, he was nonetheless a complex individual who had good qualities as well. Wozniak pointed out that Jobs softened when he did finally settle down to raise a family in his later years. The "unwanted" boy who tried hard to be a special person no longer felt the need to prove that to everyone else. His children, including the daughter he had with Brennan, became close to him. He surpassed his biological father in doing what he could not by letting go of his selfishness, giving himself to others and relaxing his control over them. "I saw that change, I was there during those days, and from then on Steve wasn't the person he'd been before we had started Apple [ . . . ] he ended up with a wife and a family and a home. He spent a lot of time there and had good relationships with his family. So, he did manage to have a side of his life that kind of didn't matter so much [ to him ] when he was younger and starting to get rich."

We can make many grandiose claims about Jobs: he was a Caesar of the modern age, a genius who dominated the world with a magnificent imagination that forever changed the world. But he was also a cruel taskmaster, a liar, a thief, and a person who undervalued others. No one can know for sure what was in his heart, but he was a magnificent individual to the end, enduring an agonizing battle with cancer and persisting with inhuman strength and self-reliance. We certainly could not say that Jobs was a "good" man.

But he was great one.

Printed in Great Britain
by Amazon

16321955R00020